# JUNIOR BIOGRAPHIES

**Therese M. Shea**

# LUPITA NYONG'O

## OSCAR-WINNING ACTRESS

**Enslow Publishing**
101 W. 23rd Street
Suite 240
New York, NY 10011
USA
enslow.com

**affirmation**  The act of saying that something is true in a confident way.

**critic**  A person who gives opinions about books, movies, or other forms of art.

**discriminate**  To unfairly treat a person or group of people differently from other people.

**documentary**  A movie that tells the facts about actual people and events.

**HIV**  The virus that causes a disease of the immune system called AIDS.

**inspire**  To make someone want to do something.

**mixed martial arts**  A sport that allows a wide range of fighting methods, including striking and kicking.

**nominate**  To choose someone as a candidate for receiving an honor or award.

**volunteer**  To offer to do something without getting paid for it.

# CONTENTS

Lupita Nyong'o

# CHAPTER 1

# INTERNATIONAL CHILDHOOD

The rise of Hollywood star Lupita Nyong'o has been fast. Her first major movie role out of school earned her an Oscar. She quickly became known for her acting skills as well as her fashion sense. But Lupita knows what is most important to her. She wants to find challenging roles on screen and support causes close to her heart off screen.

## SEEKING SAFETY

Lupita's parents, Dorothy and Peter Anyang' Nyong'o, are from Kenya. Before Lupita was born, they spoke out against an unjust government in Kenya. That put their lives in danger. They moved to Mexico. Lupita was born in Mexico City on March 1, 1983. Shortly after, the family moved to New York and then finally back to Africa. Lupita spent her childhood in Kenya.

Lupita and her mother, Dorothy

Lupita speaks the Swahili, Luo, English, Italian, and Spanish languages.

## FIRST ROLE

The Nyong'o family lived in the city of Nairobi, Kenya. Lupita's father was a professor at the university. Lupita got her first big acting role when she was fourteen. She played Juliet in William Shakespeare's *Romeo and Juliet.*

When Lupita was sixteen, her family sent her back to Mexico to learn Spanish. She then decided to attend Hampshire College in Amherst, Massachusetts.

Lupita and her brother Peter attend a film premiere. The two have four other siblings.

Lupita Says:

**"I just came to life on stage [in *Romeo and Juliet*], I just loved it so much."**

During a summer vacation in Kenya, Lupita got a job on the set of the movie *The Constant Gardener*. She met actor Ralph Fiennes. Lupita told him she wanted to be an actress. He warned her it was difficult. "Only do it if you feel you cannot live without acting," he suggested. But Lupita wasn't discouraged. She graduated from college with a film degree in 2003.

# CHAPTER 2
# STARTING OUT, BREAKING THROUGH

Lupita returned to Africa. She took the role of a college student in the MTV television series *Shuga*. The show was about young Africans, but it had a special purpose. It was meant to spread awareness about HIV.

Lupita also wrote, produced, and directed a documentary called *In My Genes*. It is about Kenyans discriminating against people with albinism, a disorder that makes black people appear to have white skin.

Lupita returned to the United States to study at the Yale School of Drama. Before she graduated in 2012, she found out that she got a part in a movie called *12 Years a Slave*. She knew that it was a huge opportunity.

Lupita Says:

"I love filmmaking, but I decided to go to drama school because I thought that when I'm 60 and looking back on my life, if acting hadn't been a part of it, I would hate myself."

## SOLOMON'S STORY

The film *12 Years a Slave* is based on the true story of a free black man named Solomon Northup. He was kidnapped and sold into slavery in the 1800s. Lupita played the role of Patsey, a slave on the farm who becomes friends with Solomon. To prepare for the role, Lupita

Lupita celebrates at her Yale graduation. She appeared in many shows while she was at Yale.

More than a thousand women tried out for the role of Patsey.

read the story of Northup's life. She also learned about the lives of women slaves.

Lupita's part was difficult, especially because Patsey was treated harshly. The **critics** were amazed by Lupita's acting. She was **nominated** for many awards. She won the Oscar for Best Supporting Actress in 2014. Her role as a Hollywood star was sealed.

When Lupita accepted the Oscar for *12 Years a Slave*, she said, "I want to salute the spirit of Patsey for her guidance. And for Solomon, thank you for telling her story and your own."

# CHAPTER 3
# CHOOSING HER ROLES

In 2014, Lupita announced she would be in the film *Star Wars: The Force Awakens.* She played a computer-generated character called Maz Kanata. Lupita liked the challenge of having to act with her voice. She also liked that people had to pay attention to her words and not her looks.

In 2015, Lupita took on a new challenge. It was a stage play in New York City called *Eclipsed.* It was about five women during a war in the African nation of Liberia. Again, Lupita won the respect of critics. She was nominated for a Tony Award for Best Actress.

## A STRONG ROLE MODEL

Lupita's next major role after *12 Years a Slave* came in 2016. *Queen of Katwe* is a Disney film about a poor ten-year-old girl in Uganda. The girl dreams of a better life and becomes a chess champion. Lupita played the girl's mother, Harriet.

Lupita poses with Stormtroopers. After *12 Years a Slave*, she wanted to play a role that wasn't too similar to Patsey. Maz Kanata in *Star Wars* was totally different.

She was a strong woman who would do anything for her children. Lupita said she connected with the true story easily. She also appreciated that it was an uplifting story about Africa, which is rarely shown in Hollywood movies.

Lupita attends the Hollywood premiere of *Queen of Katwe* in 2016. She looks for roles that show many viewpoints about what it means to be African.

## BLOCKBUSTER!

In 2018, Lupita took part in the superhero film *Black Panther*. It featured a mostly black cast directed by an African American director. Chadwick Boseman played the title role, and Lupita was his love interest—and a kind of superhero herself—named Nakia. She trained for four hours a day over six weeks to prepare for the action scenes. This included learning **mixed martial arts**.

Lupita was the voice of Raksha, the wolf mother, in the 2016 movie *The Jungle Book*.

Lupita and Chadwick Boseman perform a scene in *Black Panther*. When the film came out, Lupita paid for six hundred children in her hometown in Kenya to see it.

The movie was especially exciting for black Americans. It was not only about black superheroes but also about what it means to be an African and an American. The film impressed audiences of all backgrounds and races. It made more than $360 million worldwide over its opening weekend.

Lupita Says:

"**The little Kenyan child in me leaped for joy because [*Black Panther*]'s such an affirmation.**"

# Chapter 4
# Lupita's Causes

Lupita landed on most best-dressed lists during her breakout year for *12 Years a Slave*. She likes to wear bright colors and beautiful patterns that stand out. Lupita has been on the cover of *Vogue* magazine several times. But she hasn't always been accepted as a beauty.

## Inspiring Others

Lupita remembers a time when she was told her skin was too dark to be on television. She knew that

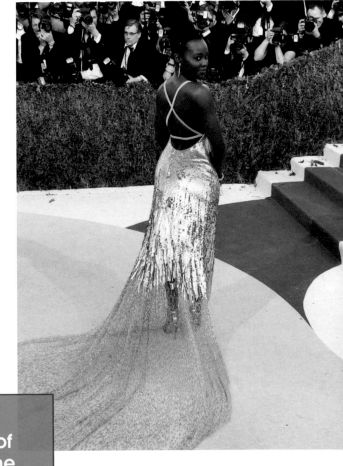

Lupita attends a benefit at the Metropolitan Museum of Art in 2016. She has become known for her style on the red carpet.

Lupita has been a strong supporter of black women wearing their hair naturally if they want to.

wasn't true and didn't let that stop her. She now speaks out to help other people accept how they look. Lupita even wrote a children's book called *Sulwe*. It is about a dark-skinned Kenyan girl who learns to accept herself. The story is **inspired** by her own childhood.

## GIVING BACK

Lupita has always been interested in helping others. She **volunteered** at an orphanage when

Lupita Says:

"Being featured on the cover of a magazine fulfills me as it is an opportunity to show other dark, kinky-haired people, and particularly our children, that they are beautiful just the way they are."

she was younger. She now works with a group called WildAid, which helps save elephants in Africa. She also supports Mother Health International. The group helps pregnant women in areas of disaster, war, and poverty. Lupita also works with young Africans who are interested in film and art careers. She says she wishes she could have talked to someone about it when she was young.

Lupita always tries to do things that are meaningful and important. She has worked hard to break down barriers and change people's views on issues that are close to her. No doubt Lupita will continue to take on challenges in her career as well as in her life.

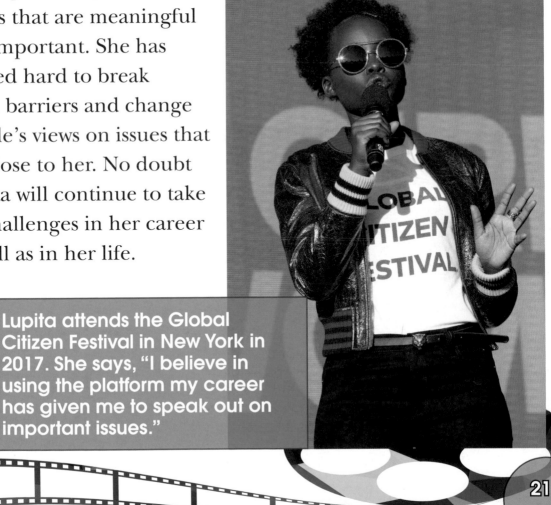

Lupita attends the Global Citizen Festival in New York in 2017. She says, "I believe in using the platform my career has given me to speak out on important issues."

# TIMELINE

**1983** Lupita Nyong'o is born on March 1 in Mexico City, Mexico.

**1999** Returns to Mexico to learn Spanish.

**2003** Graduates from Hampshire College with a film degree.

**2009** Appears in MTV's *Shuga* as Ayira.

**2009** Documentary, *In My Genes,* is released.

**2012** Graduates from Yale Drama School.

**2013** Appears as Patsey in *12 Years a Slave.*

**2014** Wins the Oscar for Best Supporting Actress for *12 Years a Slave.*

**2015** Takes a role in the stage play *Eclipsed.*

**2015** Appears as Maz Kanata in *Star Wars: The Force Awakens.*

**2016** Plays Harriet in *Queen of Katwe.*

**2017** Reprises role of Maz Kanata in *Star Wars: The Last Jedi.*

**2018** Appears as Nakia in *Black Panther.*

## BOOKS

Byers, Grace. *I Am Enough.* New York, NY: Balzer + Bray, 2018.

Furstinger, Nancy. *Today's 12 Hottest Movie Superstars.* Mankato, MN: 12 Story Library, 2015.

McCann, Jim. *Black Panther: The Junior Novel.* New York, NY: Little, Brown, 2018.

## WEBSITES

**Lupita Nyong'o Biography**
*www.biography.com/people/lupita-nyongo-21465383*
Read a short biography of Lupita.

**National Geographic Kids: Kenya**
*kids.nationalgeographic.com/explore/countries/kenya*
Learn all about Kenya, including its people, culture, and geography.

# INDEX

Published in 2020 by Enslow Publishing, LLC.
101 W. 23rd Street, Suite 240, New York, NY 10011

Copyright © 2020 by Enslow Publishing, LLC.

**Library of Congress Cataloging-in-Publication Data**
Names: Shea, Therese M., author.
Title: Lupita Nyong'o : Oscar-winning actress / Therese M. Shea.
Description: New York : Enslow Publishing, 2020. | Series: Junior biographies | Audience: Grade 3-5. | Includes bibliographical references and index.
Identifiers: LCCN 2018041872| ISBN 9781978507920 (library bound) | ISBN 9781978508897 (paperback) | ISBN 9781978508903 (6 pack)
Subjects: LCSH: Nyong'o, Lupita—Juvenile literature. | Motion picture actors and actresses—Biography.
Classification: LCC PN2287.N96 S54 2019 | DDC 791.4302/8092 [B] —dc23
LC record available at https://lccn.loc.gov/2018041872

Printed in the United States of America

**To Our Readers:** We have done our best to make sure all website addresses in this book were active and appropriate when we went to press. However, the author and the publisher have no control over and assume no liability for the material available on those websites or on any websites they may link to. Any comments or suggestions can be sent by e-mail to customerservice@enslow.com.

**Photos Credits:** Cover, p. 1 Loic Vanance/AFP/Getty Images; p. 4 Dimitrios Kambouris/Getty Images; p. 6 icphotos548645/Newscom; p. 8 Sipa USA via AP; p. 11 © AP Images; p. 13 Kevin Winter/Getty Images; p. 15 Todd Williamson/Getty Images; p. 16 Jeffrey Mayer/WireImage/Getty Images; p. 18 Album/Alamy Stock Photo; p. 19 Timothy A. Clary/AFP/Getty Images; p. 20 Phillip Faraone/Getty Images; p. 21 Greg Allen/Invision/AP; interior page bottoms (film reels) thenatchdl/Shutterstock.com.